Chinese New Year For Kids

Speedy Publishing LLC
40 E. Main St. #1156
Newark, DE 19711
www.speedypublishing.com

Chinese New Year is an important Chinese festival celebrated at the turn of the Chinese calendar.

Chinese New Year is centuries old and gains significance because of several myths and traditions. The festival was a time to honour deities as well as ancestors.

大吉大利
財源廣進

Chinese New Year is celebrated in countries and territories with significant Chinese populations. Hong Kong, Taiwan, Singapore, Indonesia and the Philippines are only a few.

福
福

Chinese New Year symbolizes letting go of the past and welcoming a new beginning.

A reunion dinner, named as “Nian Ye Fan”, is held on New Year’s Eve during which family members gather for celebration.

招

Dragon and lion dances are common during Chinese New Year. Dancers dress up as lions and dragons and perform for onlookers.

Firecrackers are often let off during Chinese New Year. They are thought to scare off evil spirits.

The first day of the New Year falls between 21 January and 20 February. Chinese New Year is the longest festival in the Chinese calendar.

吉祥
賀

Decorations generally convey a New Year greeting. Chinese calligraphy posters show Chinese idioms.

A day where Chinese
families gather for their
annual reunion dinner
is known as “Evening
of the Passing”.

www.ingramcontent.com/pod-product-compliance
Lightning Source LLC
LaVergne TN
LVHW060513170826
845677LV00026B/1734

9798869450227